pocket
cornwall

Exploring the Fowey Valley

Paul Lightfoot

Alison Hodge

First published in 2011 by
Alison Hodge, 2 Clarence Place, Penzance,
Cornwall TR18 2QA, UK
info@alison-hodge.co.uk
www.alison-hodge.co.uk

ISBN-13 978-0-906720-78-3
British Library Cataloguing-in-Publication Data
A catalogue record for this book is available from
the British Library.

Designed and originated by
BDP – Book Development and Production,
Penzance, Cornwall

Printed in China

Title page: A kayak going down the River Lerryn

Acknowledgements
Thanks to the owners of the Boconnoc
Estate, Botelet Farm and Headland Garden
for their kind permission to reproduce the
photographs on pages 7, 57, 68 and 77;
to the respective vicars to reproduce the
photographs of the church interiors on pages
7, 24, 29, 37, 65, 73 and 81, and to Sue
Lightfoot for preparing the index.

Contents

Introduction

From its source 300 metres (984 ft) above the sea in the marshes of Bodmin Moor, the River Fowey follows a winding course for 25 miles (40 km), southwards through the Draynes Valley, west through the Glynn Valley, then southwards again to its estuary and the town that bears its name. With its tributaries, the Fowey Valley covers an area of 68 square miles (177 sq km), a significant proportion of the middle part of Cornwall.

The name Fowey originates from the Cornish word *fawi*, meaning beech trees. The valley is a beautiful and fascinating place. It encompasses some of the best of Cornwall's countryside, and much of the county's natural and human history is embedded within the landscape.

Start with the wildlife. The valleys of the River Fowey, its tributaries and their watersheds include eight areas designated by Natural England as Sites of Special Scientific Interest (SSSIs). Probably the best known and most visited is Draynes Wood, which includes the Golitha Falls National Nature Reserve.

A waterfall at Golitha Falls, high on the River Fowey

Evidence of human activity on Bodmin Moor dates from the Bronze Age. The valley includes the sites of five Iron Age castles and two from the Norman period. Most of them are on hilltops and offer superb views of the surrounding countryside. Restormel Castle is surely the most impressive, on its commanding site above the river a mile (2 km) north of Lostwithiel.

Our area has some fine old buildings. Lanhydrock and Boconnoc are among Cornwall's best-known estates. And we will visit 12 churches, each with its particular architectural style, some imposing within the towns and villages they serve, others hidden at the end of lanes in obscure valleys, and most of them lovingly maintained by dedicated groups of volunteers. In his book *England's Thousand Best Churches*, Simon Jenkins included four from the Fowey Valley: St Neot, St Winnow, Lanteglos and St Sampson's; others might just as well have qualified. There is always something magical about pushing open the heavy door of a country church with no-one else about, and peering over empty pews at stone fonts and carved wood that bear the marks of craftsmen who lived hundreds of years ago.

The estuary is one of Cornwall's best-known centres for sailing and cultural events. Yet there are plenty of surprises hidden in its tidal creeks, whose beauty, mysteries and history have found their way into the works of some of the county's leading literary figures.

Sir Arthur Quiller-Couch lived in Fowey, and wrote about the town in his novels and short stories. Kenneth Grahame was a frequent visitor, and drew inspiration from the area for the children's classic *The Wind in the Willows*. The best known of Fowey's writers is Daphne du Maurier, who lived most of her life on or near the estuary. Her Cornish novels include many local landmarks, and bring local history to life.

The Fowey Valley is highly accessible. Intricate networks of bridleways and footpaths crisscross the countryside from the moors to the estuary, providing numerous opportunities for circular or point-to-point walking, from casual strolls to demanding hikes. From Lostwithiel to the sea there are several places to launch or hire kayaks and small boats.

Paul Lightfoot, 2011

Facing page: The wagon roof of St Wyllow Church, Lanteglos (left). A sailing boat leaving the estuary of the River Fowey, viewed from Headland Gardens, Polruan (right)

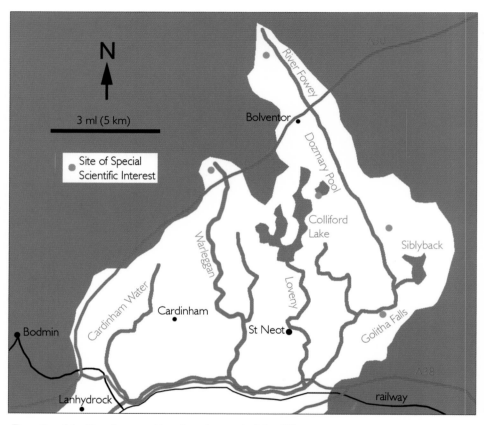

The valley of the River Fowey and its tributaries: north of the A38

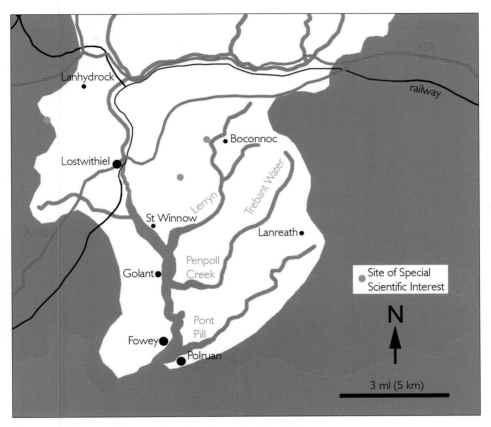

Lanhydrock

railway

Boconnoc

Lostwithiel

Lerryn

Trebant Water

St Winnow

Lanreath

Golant

Penpoll
Creek

Pont
Pill

Fowey

Polruan

Site of Special
Scientific Interest

N

3 ml (5 km)

The valley of the River Fowey and its tributaries: south of the A38

The Upper Reaches of the River Fowey

The River Fowey rises in a shallow, marshy basin to the west of Buttern Hill on Bodmin Moor, with the top of Brown Willy, the highest point in Cornwall, visible to the southwest. As a moorland stream it winds its way past Leskernick and Codda Downs, and under the A30 trunk road at Palmersbridge. It follows an almost straight course for six miles (9 km) to Draynes Bridge near Golitha Falls. Here it turns towards the west, flows under the fifteenth-century Treverbyn Bridge, and enters the Glynn Valley.

Three tributaries also flow off the moor: the Loveny, or St Neot River, passes through the artificial Colliford Lake; to the west is the Warleggan or Bedalder River, which rises near Hawk's Tor, and still further west is Cardinham Water.

Fowey Well under Brown Willy on Bodmin Moor

Windswept trees and granite boulders, Leskernick Hill (left). Bluebells line the bank of the young River Fowey (right)

Bodmin Moor

Bodmin Moor was originally known as Fowey Moor, or Fawimor, named for its principal river, as are its neighbours to the east, Dartmoor and Exmoor. The modern name seems to have been introduced when the first Ordnance Survey (OS) maps were prepared early in the nineteenth century.

Bodmin Moor dominates much of central Cornwall. It originated from a massive intrusion of molten rock that was forced upwards from deep within the earth's crust, and which cooled to form principally granite with its distinctive crystalline texture. The heat of the intruded rocks created a boundary of highly metamorphosed slates and shales around what is now the moor. Extensive mineral deposits formed within the granite, including tin and copper, with occasional traces of iron, lead, silver and zinc.

The modern landscape is one of gentle, almost treeless slopes strewn with boulders, and craggy granite outcrops on the hilltops. It is a landscape that both natural and human-induced processes have helped to create.

Periglacial erosion during the Ice Ages scoured vertical and horizontal striations in the exposed granite, and left screes on some of the slopes. Soils formed from the granite are coarse and acid, with a surface layer of peat that is shallow on the slopes and deeper in the bogs and marshes of the valleys.

The natural vegetation of the upper slopes is heath and grassland with richer, more complex communities where surface water occurs. Deciduous trees grow in the courses of the streams, often supporting epiphytic lichens. A variety of sphagnum mosses have colonized the bogs, together with a number of flowering plants. There are rare orchids as well as the more common cotton grass and the bluebells that carpet the stream banks in April and May each year.

Otters have been observed in the upper reaches of the River Fowey, but the area is better known for its birds. It is a breeding area for the curlew, lapwing, redstart, snipe, stonechat and wheatear. Small numbers of hen harriers, merlins, peregrines and red kites visit in the winter, together with the more common short-eared owl and golden plover. The moor is important for dragonfly, damselfly and some scarce butterfly species.

Thousands of years of extensive grazing have affected the balance of plant species on the upper slopes of the moor, resulting in semi-natural rather than natural vegetation. More recently the numbers of grazing animals have declined and gorse, bracken and ferns have become more widespread. This change in the balance of the vegetation has restricted access in parts of the moor and hidden some archaeological features.

Nevertheless, with the help of the OS map it is possible to make out the remains of early human settlement near the source of the River Fowey. Ancient stone cairns mark the tops of the nearby hills, and about 50 Bronze Age hut circles and field boundaries line the western and southern slopes of Leskernick Hill. While they may be difficult

Bodmin Moor: Moorland cattle graze by the River Fowey near its source (left). Leskernick Farm with Fowey Valley in the background (right)

to pick out on the ground, the OS map and Google Earth's satellite photographs show a series of clearly identifiable circles and oblongs.

Recently, archaeologists found that Leskernick Quoit – a flat stone 2 m wide, supported by three vertical stones – points almost directly to the setting sun on 21 June, when viewed from a burial mound on the nearby Beacon Hill. Calculations showed that the alignment would have been perfect during the early Neolithic period, around 3600 BC.

There are clear signs too of tin streaming. Prospectors diverted water-courses to wash out the tin and copper that was embedded in the rocks and soils. The resulting scarring of the landscape remains especially prominent

between Buttern and Leskernick Hills, and the courses of leats can still be seen following the contours of the valley.

The source of the River Fowey is difficult to pinpoint exactly. Fowey Well on the eastern slopes of Brown Willy has sometimes been claimed as the start of the river. It seems conveniently precise and is the highest point from which permanent or intermittent streams can be traced. But a network of small streams in the marshes about half a mile (1 km) to the north is further from the river mouth and is marked as the source on the OS map.

Walkers may reach the area from the bridleway near Codda in the south, then turning north to cross open moorland near Leskernick, one of Bodmin Moor's most

The A30 where it crosses the River Fowey, with Jamaica Inn on the skyline (left). Jamaica Inn today (right)

isolated farmhouses that was occupied till recently. Alternatively, follow the bridleway south-west from Carne Down, or walk in from New Park or Bowithick to the north.

Whatever the route, take sensible precautions, especially in uncertain weather. What seems a safe, clear footpath can peter out in a treacherous bog, resulting in, at best, an unpleasant wet-footed trudge in search of firmer ground. At worst there are stories, perhaps apocryphal, of people and even vehicles disappearing without trace. The US Army trained here during the Second World War; according to a farmer whom Wilson Macarthur quotes in his 1948 book *The River Fowey*, a personnel carrier took a wrong turn, sank slowly, and was said to be still submerged somewhere beneath the bog.

Jamaica Inn and Bolventor

The river passes under the A30 at Palmersbridge, from which the village of Bolventor and its far more famous local pub, Jamaica Inn, can be seen on the crest of the hill to the south-west.

Jamaica Inn was built in the eighteenth century as a staging post for travellers crossing the moor between Launceston and Bodmin, and Bolventor village grew up around it. As for a Jamaican connection, the inn might have served as a hiding or trading place for liquor smuggled into the country, including rum from the Caribbean.

Bolventor Church and churchyard (left). Cattle grazing on a hillside near Siblyback, Bodmin Moor (right)

During the winter of 1930, Daphne du Maurier and her friend Foy Quiller-Couch stayed at the inn while exploring Bodmin Moor on horseback. They thought the inn 'hospitable and kindly,' according to a note at the start of the novel that du Maurier eventually wrote, but they found the moor a desolate, fog-bound and sometimes frightening place. One afternoon they got lost and had to rely on the horses' instincts to find their way back to safety. Du Maurier used these experiences, together with a cast of dark characters, in her fourth novel, *Jamaica Inn*, which was published in 1936.

The modern Jamaica Inn is still buffeted by wind and rain, and blanketed by the mists that du Maurier described; and occasionally it takes in travellers who have been trapped by snow on the highway. Alongside its hotel and restaurant, Jamaica Inn has a Daphne du Maurier memorial room; a museum of the smugglers, pirates and wreckers that the novel depicts; a shop that sells du Maurier memorabilia, and a good line in ghosts and murder stories. There is a nice irony in a place made famous for its remote, dark, mysterious and possibly criminal past becoming a modern, well-branded tourist attraction.

A little to the east of the inn and across the A30 lies Bolventor Church, consecrated in 1848 and dedicated to the Holy Trinity. The churchyard is still used and well maintained, but not the church. From a distance, the small, well-proportioned Gothic building retains a certain elegance, and must once have been a source of local pride. But it fell into

The Draynes Valley: Cattle and wildflowers at Dozmary Hill Farm (left). Reeds near Wimalford (right)

disuse in the 1990s and its windows have been boarded up; the door is locked and chained, and the slates are slipping from the roof.

The Draynes Valley

South of the A30, the valley widens to include a flood plain as far south as Lamelgate, where the narrowing valley was once considered a possible site for a dam. Here the landscape is less wild than on the moor. Much of the valley is criss-crossed by stone walls enclosing livestock pastures; a minor road from Bolventor to Redgate follows the western bank of the river. Nevertheless, like Bodmin Moor, this area has valuable flora and fauna, and 124 ha (306 acres) have been notified as a SSSI.

The flood plain has a variety of plant communities, including heath and grassland, with many wildflowers and willow and oak trees near the stream. Colonies of the invasive Japanese knotweed occur on the river banks. Otters have been recorded on this stretch of the river, which the Fowey River Association maintains as a breeding sanctuary for salmon and trout.

Breeding birds here include the attractive but difficult-to-find kingfisher, redstarts, stonechats, tree pipits and winchats, and a number of species of warblers. Below Nine Stones and Wimalford is good for bird watching.

Hut circles and field systems on the higher slopes of the valley, on Browngelly Downs to the west and Hilltor Downs to the east, are evidence of early settlement and farming. Most of today's farms had medieval origins, including Harrowbridge, Higher and Lower Langdon, Wimalford, Westerlake, Furswain and Lamelgate. There is evidence of alluvial tin works along the banks of the river between Higher and Lower Langdon, and the remains of tin mining near Goodaver.

At Trekeivesteps, a small tributary flows into the River Fowey from Siblyback Lake, which was created in 1969 to provide water for the towns and villages of south-east Cornwall. It is now owned and operated by South West Water, but is better known as a centre for outdoor watersports.

Golitha Falls

For 800 m downstream from the Draynes Bridge, the River Fowey cascades through a narrow gorge and over a series of rapids known collectively as the Golitha Falls. The name is believed to come from an old Cornish word for 'obstruction', because a giant boulder almost blocked the river before it was blown up sometime in the nineteenth century. Shaded by dense woodland yet easily accessible, this is one of the most distinctive and best-known stretches of the entire course of the river.

Golitha Falls is a National Nature Reserve (NNR), one of about 220 in England, and one of only 35 designated as particularly significant 'Spotlight' NNRs. For scientists, the Golitha NNR is noted for its stands of oak, ash and beech that were once part of a larger area of ancient woodland. Holly, hazel and a rare variety of fern occur on the forest floor.

There are also lichens and several varieties of rare mosses and liverworts – small non-flowering, spore-producing plants of which about 50 varieties have been recorded on the damp soil or rotting logs within the Golitha NNR.

Evidence of human activity dates from the early Norman period when coppice management was practised in the woodlands. Coppicing is an ancient technique whereby trees are regularly cut a little above the ground in order to bring on a regular supply of timber without having to replant. Coppicing creates 'coppice stools' – rings of trunks from a common set of roots; we will find more examples later, around the estuary. For part

Facing page: The River Fowey cascades over rapids at the Golitha Falls

A line of mature beech trees on the bank of the River Fowey at Golitha Falls

of its length the footpath follows the line of a planted avenue of majestic, mature beech trees that line the river bank.

Within the Golitha NNR are the remains of a number of mine workings, including the Wheal Victoria copper mine. There are two waterwheel pits that were dug into the rocks on the river bank above the falls; and nearby mine drainage tunnels have been colonized by bats. An iron pipe near the entrance to the woods once carried waste from china clay workings in the neighbouring St Neot valley.

Access to much of the area was improved in 1993 to facilitate the filming of a scene for the Disney version of *The Three Musketeers*. At the time of writing, Natural England and Cornwall Council are planning to extend the existing easy-access path so that disabled

Bluebells beside the ancient, leaf-covered Treverbyn Bridge over the River Fowey

visitors may see more of the falls. The area is open throughout the year, and the falls are at their most spectacular shortly after periods of heavy rain.

After Golitha the river follows a serene, wooded and rather inaccessible course to its confluence with the Trenant stream which flows down from Park Pit, the site of flooded china clay works that was absorbed into the South West Water network in 2008 and has no public access.

For about 500 m the river bank forms part of the Two Valleys Walk from St Neot, which we come to later. From there it flows under the picturesque fifteenth-century Treverbyn Bridge, past Ashford Mill, under the A38 and on to Two Waters Foot where it meets its first significant tributary, the River Loveny.

The River Loveny

Bodmin Moor: Reeds by Dozmary Pool (left); foxgloves beside Colliford Lake (right)

Of the five lakes in the upper reaches of the valley of the River Fowey and its tributaries, Dozmary Pool is the only natural one. With a surface area of 15 ha (37 acres), it is set in a shallow, gently sloping basin between Browngelly and Dozmary Downs, a little more than a mile (2 km) south from Bolventor. It is well above the level of the River Fowey but drains to the west into the River Loveny, also known as the St Neot River.

It takes quite a stretch of the imagination to be impressed by Dozmary Pool, in spite of its prominent place in Arthurian legend. This is supposedly where King Arthur rowed out to receive the sword Excalibur from the Lady of the Lake, and where the sword was returned when Arthur died. The lake was said to be bottomless.

In fact, Dozmary Pool is quite shallow, and has occasionally dried out completely during prolonged periods of drought. It is a small fraction of the size of the nearby artificial Colliford Lake, and except when the winter mists descend its setting does little to conjure up any sense of the mystery that legends suggest. Dozmary Pool's present significance lies

A stone bridge below the Colliford Dam on the River Loveny

more in its protected status as a SSSI, notified for the dwarf shrub heath and bog on its southern shore.

Like Siblyback, Colliford is owned and operated by South West Water. Extending nearly three miles (5 km) from north to south, it is by far the largest inland body of water in central Cornwall. Created in 1986 by damming the seemingly tiny River Loveny,

it can provide two-thirds of the public water requirements of the entire county. It has also become an attractive and accessible recreation area, especially for walkers and strollers for whom the higher and more remote parts of Bodmin Moor may be too demanding.

Fishing is allowed, with a permit, and Colliford is promoted as having some of Cornwall's best traditional fly-fishing for

St Neot Church: The tower with its oak branch (left); a stained glass window depicting Noah and scenes from the biblical flood (right)

natural brown trout. Near its northern end is Colliford Lake Park, which offers indoor and outdoor play and picnic areas, nature trails and petting animals, and arranges occasional musical and other events. There is a small nature reserve on the eastern shore.

From the dam the river flows by 'open access' land half a mile (1 km) through a steep-sided, narrow band of woodland bordering Great and Little Hamnett farms, under a bridge carrying the lane to Trewindle and Trevenna, before winding south to St Neot.

St Neot

Though it is home to only 400 people, St Neot is the largest settlement in the upper reaches of the valley of the River Fowey and its tributaries. It lies in the steep-sided, wooded valley of the River Loveny on what was once the main road between Bodmin and Liskeard. Its London Inn was a regular stopping place for travellers.

Standing next to the inn, the church dominates the village and is best known for its sixteenth-century stained glass windows – 'the principal treasure of Cornish religious art' according to Simon Jenkins – depicting scenes from the Genesis version of the creation, among other biblical events, and the life of St Neot.

Oddly, the branch of an oak tree extends from the roof of the bell tower. The villagers replace the oak branch in a ceremony on 29 May each year in memory of a request from King Charles I to celebrate the village's support for the Royalist cause during the English Civil War.

St Neot was selected as England's Village of the Year in 2004 in a contest that emphasized the extent and quality of community life, facilities and activities. Two years later St

A roadsign at Crowpound Cross, near St Neot

Neot was further honoured as the Village of the Decade in a contest commemorating the tenth anniversary of the competition.

St Neot makes a good centre for hikers. The circular Two Valleys Walk passes up the valley of the Loveny and eastwards around the northern edge of Berry Down before descending to the valley of the River Fowey.

At the top of Berry Down, a short diversion south from the Two Valleys Walk, are the remains of Berry Castle which dates back at least to the Iron Age. The inner ramparts are readily identifiable, although it is difficult for the casual visitor to make sense of the granite blocks and earthworks, partly overgrown, that lie within them. In the spring, both the remains of the castle and the slopes beyond are covered with extensive, beautiful

Earthworks of an Iron Age castle on Berry Down, near St Neot

stands of foxgloves. And as with most hill-top castles, on a clear day the views over the surrounding countryside fully repay the effort of the climb.

From Berry Down, the route follows the course of the Trenant stream to a delightful stretch of about 500 m on the bank of the River Fowey above Treverbyn Bridge. The walk returns along the lanes to St Neot.

Footpaths from the village also lead west to Goonzion Downs, which is peppered with small pits dug by mineral prospectors, and south along the course of the River Loveny to Carnglaze. Here the caverns quarried into the dramatically dark, glossy slate are fascinating in themselves; they are also used as a centre for local fairs and musical events.

The Warleggan River

Hawk's Tor and Hawk's Tor Pit on the Warleggan tributary of the River Fowey

The River Fowey's second main tributary, the Warleggan or Bedalder River, rises to the east of Hawk's Tor and about half a mile (1 km) north of the A30. It passes Hawk's Tor Pit, the small hamlet of Temple and the village for which it is named before flowing south to join the River Fowey in the Glynn Valley.

Hawk's Tor Pit marks the remains of some old china clay workings that have flooded to form a small lake which is visible from

Temple

Few of the Fowey Valley's attractions have as intriguing a history as the little church of St Catherine at Temple. Temple is a tiny hamlet of fewer than 30 modern inhabitants, on the side of the valley of the Warleggan River soon after it passes under the A30. If the A30 had been built in a straight line following the old turnpike from Launceston to Bodmin it would have sliced the village in half, and the church might have suffered the same fate as its nearest neighbour to the north-east at Bolventor.

The original church and a nearby abbey are believed to have been built in about 1120 by the Knights Templar, and served as a place of rest for travellers, including pilgrims crossing between the north and south coasts of the peninsula. An old packhorse road from Camelford to Liskeard passed close to the church. After the suppression of the Knights Templar in the fourteenth century, their lands and property passed to the Knights Hospitaller, and after the Reformation to the Crown.

It was not until 1744 that Temple Church was fully incorporated into the formal structures of the Church of England. While it

A moorland road near Temple, Bodmin Moor

the A30. A SSSI extends for 6 ha (15 acres) around the northern edge of the pit, notified for the pollen and other organic deposits revealed in vertical soil and rock profiles. These sediments provide a detailed record of vegetation and climatic changes over the last 13,000 years.

St Catherine's Church, Temple (above and right)

remained outside the Bishop's jurisdiction, Temple was managed by independent-minded curates who, among other irregularities, carried out marriages without issuing banns or licences, and Temple gained a slightly scandalous reputation as a Cornish Gretna Green. As the eighteenth century historian Thomas Tonkin put it, 'many a bad marriage bargain is there yearly slubbered up.'

During the following hundred years the church fell into disuse, and its roof and walls collapsed. In a heroic act of community service, the rector, JR Brown, and a small group of local residents rebuilt the church on the original foundations in 1882, creating what they claimed was one of the handsomest churches in Cornwall. On May Day 1883 it was reopened at a ceremony attended by the Bishop and an estimated 2,000 people – an astonishing number for such a small and remote hamlet.

Since then the fortunes and condition of the church have continued to fluctuate. In 1996, a visitor found it 'dirty, damp, not quite derelict but obviously disused and sadly neglected,' and wrote in the visitors' book

Wooda Bridge over the Warleggan River, near Warleggan

that she was 'sad to see a part of our Templar heritage so sadly neglected. It could be a beautiful gem.'

Fortunately, by 2010 'a beautiful gem' would again be a fair description, and recent visitors' book entries describe it as 'peaceful', 'serene', 'special' and 'a haven'. The modern Temple Church is well worth a visit, and a contribution.

Warleggan

After Temple, the river follows an irregular winding course southward, crossed by few footpaths and no roads until the elegant nineteenth-century bridge at Wooda, about half a mile (1 km) from the village that gives the river its name. This tiny community also

Snowdrops in the churchyard at Warleggan

gave its name to one of the main characters in Winston Graham's series of Poldark novels. The connection brings a few visitors each year to what John Betjeman described as this 'desolate and almost deserted village', although the coincidence of the names is the only link between the village and the books.

Warleggan's main attraction is its church, dedicated to St Bartholomew. Parts of the building can be traced to the thirteenth century, though there have been several changes since then. The most dramatic occurred in 1818, when lightning destroyed the spire and all the stained glass. Two of the three bells had to be sold to pay for repairs to the tower, and new windows were fitted in the late nineteenth and early twentieth centuries. The spire has never been rebuilt.

All signs of damage are now long gone, and the church has a pleasingly open and welcoming interior. A large plaque commemorates local support for the King during the Civil War. More touching is the dedication of a pair of stained glass windows to the then rector's only son, who served as a soldier in Burma and died there in 1909. Both the church and its extended churchyard are well maintained and, as usual, we find generous comments in the visitors' book.

'A little treasure', 'It was lovely to be able to come and sit for a while', and even 'A lifelong ambition achieved', say visitors from all over England and Europe, and as far away as Japan and Australia. But the rather cryptic, 'Had to come and see where once there were cardboard cut-outs' needs some explanation.

It relates to surely the strangest character in the church's history, Frederick Densham, who served as rector from 1931 till his death in 1951. His strong views, autocratic nature, sympathies with the Methodists and eccentric behaviour led to a spectacular falling out with his parish council and the local community. The congregation eventually refused to attend his services, whereupon Densham filled the pews with cardboard effigies and preached to them instead.

Daphne du Maurier wrote about the village, the church and its most famous rector in her non-fiction work *Vanishing Cornwall* (1967). John Betjeman made a number of visits with his family, and recorded his impressions in his book *Cornwall* (1934).

A track leads south from Warleggan and joins the river for almost half a mile (1 km) to the pretty fifteenth-century Pantersbridge, which is too narrow and weak to carry present-day traffic and has been bypassed by a more modern structure. From the bridge, a lane continues to the south, following a picturesque stretch of the river past the Environment Agency's Trengoffe river-gauging station and its weir.

With records since 1969, this humble facility – the only one for Bodmin Moor – is part of a national network of stations on rivers that are unaffected by artificially induced changes in water flows. They provide key information about changes in rainfall, peak levels of water flow and flood risks.

The lane south from Pantersbridge meets a bridleway that crosses the river and turns back towards the north, making a pleasant circular walk. The river flows on towards the south and its confluence with the River Fowey a little downstream from the Halfway House pub at Drawbridge.

Cardinham Water

Cardinham from Bury Castle, with Cardinham Woods in the distance

Cardinham Water starts as a tiny stream below the firing range on Cardinham Moor, and is joined by several other minor watercourses that drain the area to the south and east of the A30. This area is primarily of farmland, but it includes patches of moorland on Treslea and Cardinham Downs, and Cardinham Woods – one of the largest woodlands in Cornwall. There are treasures along its networks of lanes, bridleways and footpaths.

Bury Castle

Moss-covered stone hedges beside the lane leading to Bury Castle

The first is Bury Castle, the remains of an Iron Age settlement that overlooks the village of Cardinham. It can be reached by following the bridleway from Treslea Downs towards Higher Bury, then turning left on a narrow footpath that leads up to the castle between two ancient-looking stone hedges covered with a thick layer of almost luminous green moss. The path itself rises gently enough, but the land falls away steeply below the eastern side of the outer ramparts.

The two-metre (7 ft)-high inner ramparts make a nearly complete circle, steep on the outside but sloping gently inwards to a flat, well-grazed area broken by a few large stones scattered in no clear pattern on the southern side. The only vegetation aside from the short grass consists of a few gorse bushes and short, skeletal trees. The outer slopes of the ramparts on the south-west and western sides are bordered by a dry stone wall, in places three metres (10 ft) high from the outside, and a formidable barrier for anyone who struggled up the hill and tried to enter from those directions.

But it is not certain that defence was the main function of these hilltop sites. Archaeologists now regard them as centres for trading, ceremonies and festivals, perhaps without any permanent residential or defensive purpose. It is easy to see why this site would have been an attractive place for public gatherings and celebrations. The view extends over the moors as far as Caradon Hill nine miles (14 km) to the east, and to the south and west over beautiful, rolling countryside, sunlit if you are lucky and as uplifting now as it would have been for those who built the castle more than 2,000 years ago.

Cardinham

Trees encircle the remains of the castle at Cardinham, under a stormy sky

Just over a mile (2 km) to the south is a castle with a very different history. Cardinham Castle is on private land, but its remains can be seen to the east and above the bridleway that passes nearby. The castle was built in 1080 by Richard Fitz Turold and follows the motte (mound) and bailey (enclosure) design typical of many defensive structures built by the Normans soon after their conquest of England. As invaders, defence against the people whose land had been seized would have been an important consideration. The castle might once have included a wooden structure, but all that remains is a series of steep-sided earthworks and a grassy hollow encircled by trees. From the castle there are good views to the north beyond the village of Cardinham.

The family changed its name to that of the local community, and the Cardinhams lived at the castle for about 100 years before leaving it for a more impressive home to the south at Restormel, which we will come to soon.

The name Cardinham is thought to have been derived from two Celtic words, *caer* and *dinan*, meaning 'castle' and 'fortress' respectively. Could this mean that the village was initially named for the much older structure that we now know as Bury Castle, which is visible on the skyline to the north-east? The modern village has a Methodist chapel, a primary school, an accredited campsite and a village hall, but the church is its outstanding feature.

St Meubred's Church

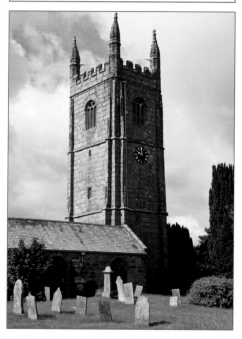

St Meubred's Church, Cardinham

The church is dedicated to St Meubred, an Irish priest who lived here in the fifth century. There have probably been other, smaller churches on the same site, but the present building dates from the fifteenth century. The impressively large church has a three-stage tower that houses a set of bells and a chiming clock. But St Meubred's and its churchyard are remarkable for a number of features.

The churchyard has two ancient stone crosses, one tall and weather-beaten beside the entrance gate, and one facing the entrance to the church; this latter cross is thought to be 1,200 years old, and is considered to be one of the finest Celtic crosses in Cornwall. Inside there is a Norman font, and near the north door a smaller replacement, installed when the original was temporarily lost. The carved ends to most of the benches date from the fifteenth century. In the southeast corner of the church is a large plaque dating from the seventeenth century, commemorating members of the Glynn family.

In January 1942, a stray bomb landed near the church and destroyed the large stained glass windows on the eastern wall. The new windows, installed in 1948, were designed by one of England's best-known stained glass artists of the time, Geoffrey Webb, whose distinctive monogram may be seen in a panel at the bottom of the right-most window.

The visitors' book is revealing, as usual. Like so many country churches, St Meubred's engenders feelings of peace, tranquillity,

St Meubred's Church, Cardinham: Glynn family memorial (left); fifteenth-century bench end (middle); monogram of Geoffrey Webb on the east window (right)

serenity, quiet beauty and a sense of history and of homecoming for those tracking down their ancestors. 'We found this lovely peace on just the right day,' Rosemary and Loveday tell us; 'We don't have this kind of history,' says a lady from New York. Newly arrived members of the community introduce themselves. There are thanks for the Friends of St Meubred's, who keep the church open and so well maintained. A few visitors admit to being driven in by the rain, but more ominously a man from northern England reports being 'charged by a field of aggressive cows.'

Cardinham Woods

Two footpaths lead from the village down to Cardinham Water which, after about half a mile (1 km) or so, flows into a large area of woodlands known collectively as Cardinham Woods. The Forestry Commission manages the timber-cutting and tree-planting operations, and has made the woods into an attractive recreation area.

The mixed deciduous and coniferous woods cover 250 ha (about 620 acres),

The clapper bridge over Cardinham Water, Cardinham Woods

including some steep-sided valleys criss-crossed by Forestry tracks suitable for walking, biking or horse-riding. Among many possible routes, the Commission has identified and signposted four circular walks, each graded as easy or moderate, except for the 'strenuous' climb up to the remains of the old Wheal Glynn silver mine. The mine closed in the 1890s and the engine house and its castellated, ivy-clad chimney have been almost consumed by the trees and undergrowth.

The Commission arranges events to encourage children to develop an interest in the environment and wildlife. Among the more

Cardinham Woods: Cardinham Water (left); the ivy-clad chimney of the Wheal Glynn mine (right)

notable and attractive species in the area are deer, buzzards, otters and kingfishers. Part of Callywith Wood is reserved for a study of the dormouse, an 'indicator species' whose well-being provides clues to the general condition and management of local woodland habitats.

For many visitors, the most convenient approach to Cardinham Woods is from the road through Fletchersbridge to the south. The excellent Woods Café is open through-out the year.

The Glynn Valley

A CrossCountry express train passes over the East Largin Viaduct above the Glynn Valley

We saw a monument to the Glynn family in St Meubred's Church, Cardinham. The family home, Glynn House, is visible from the A38, near the turning to Bodmin Parkway station, and their name is honoured in the narrow, tree-lined section of the Fowey Valley where it flows west from Two Waters Foot to the confluence with Cardinham Water.

The Glynn Valley is most obviously a transportation route. The road that is now the A38 became the main link between Bodmin and Liskeard in the 1830s, superseding the old route through St Neot. Cutting into the sides of the valley in the narrowest sections, high enough to avoid the risk of flooding, must have been no easy task. But as a feat of engineering it cannot compare with the railway.

The main line connecting Cornwall with London opened in May 1859. It descends from 60 m above the river where it enters the Glynn Valley almost to river level at Bodmin Parkway station, along the way crossing six viaducts over deep gullies where minor streams flow north, down to the main river.

A track in sunlit woods above the Glynn Valley (above). A fallen tree inside Largin Castle (right)

The highest and longest, 46 m high and 193 m long, is the St Pinnock viaduct, above the former explosives store of Trago Mills – now a sprawling, fiercely British shopping centre.

As for each of the other viaducts, St Pinnock's original stone towers – nine of them – were designed with an angled array of heavy wooden beams at the top to carry the track. In the 1870s and 1880s a new set of towers was constructed for each viaduct, parallel to the old ones, built entirely of stone. The originals still stand beside their taller replacements, ivy-covered, forlorn, redundant.

The A38 is too busy and narrow to be recommended for walkers or cyclists, but on either side several lanes and tracks lead off and up into safer and more interesting territory.

Largin Castle

The Iron Age Largin Castle is identifiable on the ground as an island of oak trees in a sea of conifers. It can be reached from the lane that rises steeply from Bodithiel Bridge beside Trago Mills, then by taking a foresters' and dog walkers' track for about half a mile (1 km) towards the west.

Climbing up through the bracken on the castle's old ramparts and into the remains of the original structure is a struggle, rewarded by a mess of undergrowth and fallen trees and a barely discernible pattern of old earthworks. Archaeologists have identified three sets of concentric ramparts up to 3.5 m high with entrances on the southern or uphill side, though it is hard for the casual visitor to make them out. The trees block any chance of a panoramic view over the valley. The peace is occasionally broken by the hum of trains crossing the East Largin viaduct nearby.

A longhorn heifer in the Nature Reserve

The Cabilla and Redrice Nature Reserve

Nearly two miles (3 km) to the west, the slowly maturing River Fowey flows through the Cabilla and Redrice Nature Reserve, a 77 ha (190 acre) area of mainly broadleaved woodland managed by Cornwall Wildlife Trust (CWT). Footpaths lead back upstream, following the course of the river for a while before turning away and up into the narrow, steep-sided valley of a small tributary. Cabilla Wood is on the western side of the stream, with Redrice Wood to the east.

If nothing else, the Forestry tracks make for a pleasant woodland walk under a canopy of trees that occasionally opens into one of the glades created by CWT as part of its management programme. It can be muddy, so this is a place for boots rather than casual shoes. There is much of interest to look out for.

This is an ancient woodland, with a long history of oak and hazel coppicing, originally for making charcoal. For birdwatchers, the pied flycatcher nests here in the spring and summer. Visitors might find some long-horned, long-haired Highland cattle grazing among the ferns beside the track, and less easily seen are deer, otters and adders – another reason for those boots. The hazel sustains colonies of dormice. A pond provides a habitat for amphibious insects, frogs, toads and newts. And this is one of only a few

A peaceful view of the River Fowey in the Glynn Valley

sites in Devon and Cornwall where the nocturnal blue ground beetle may be found.

In the nineteenth century, a number of mine shafts – adits – were dug horizontally into the valley sides in search of tin and other metals. Long disused, locked gates prevent public access; but some of the adits are home to lesser and greater horseshoe bats.

The beautiful site of Glynn House has been occupied since the eleventh century, though the present building dates from 1805. The surrounding estate was broken up in the 1950s, and for some years the house served as the premises of the Glynn Research Institute. More recently it has been divided into private residences.

Respryn to Restormel

As the river turns towards the south, it passes first under the A38 and then under a stone viaduct that carries the railway linking the town of Bodmin with the main line at Bodmin Parkway station. Since 1986, this four-mile (6 km) spur has been maintained and developed by the Bodmin Railway Preservation Society, and is generally known as the Bodmin and Wenford line. In Bodmin it links with a line that continues into the Camel Valley. This is one of about 100 heritage railways in Britain, though few run, as this one does, on standard gauge track.

From Bodmin Parkway, a series of footpaths follow the main line and the river to Lostwithiel, an easy three-mile (5 km) walk with diversions to several points of interest.

Respryn

After about half a mile (1 km), the route crosses the river at Respryn Bridge, a much-photographed structure of which the central arch dates from the fifteenth century, though

The Bodmin and Wenford steam train coming up from Bodmin Parkway station

The old bridge at Respryn

there was a recognized fording point, a chapel and a hamlet here at least 300 years earlier. The bridge was later extended, and was the focus of a skirmish during the English Civil War in 1644, when locals helped the army of Richard Grenville secure it against a Parliamentary force led by the Earl of Essex.

Probably the venerable but narrow bridge's biggest modern enemy is the sat nav. In 2006, a 40-ton truck jammed itself between the parapets, eventually being dragged free after causing damage that cost £30,000 to repair.

Autumnal colours of a tulip tree at Respryn

Lanhydrock

Lanhydrock House is a short walk west from Respryn. The path from the river enters through the estate's lower gate and leads up to the house between a half-mile (1 km) long avenue of beech trees. Unusually in Cornwall, the owner of Lanhydrock, Lord Robartes, supported the Parliamentary side during the Civil War. He planted these impressive trees to celebrate Cromwell's victory.

Lord Robartes had completed the construction of the house in the 1630s, and it remained in the Robartes family until Viscount Clifden gave the 182-ha (450-acre) estate to the National Trust in 1953. Since then, it has become a fascinating local attraction.

Most of the house was destroyed by fire in 1881, and subsequently rebuilt. Only the northern wing escaped the blaze. Above its ground floor is the magnificent Long Gallery, which houses a large collection of rare books overlooked by a high, intricately worked seventeenth-century plaster ceiling depicting Old Testament events. Throughout the house, 50 rooms are open to the public, showing intimate glimpses into the lives of recent generations of the Robartes family, their army of servants and their kitchens.

The surrounding gardens are as impressive as the house, particularly in the spring when the camellias and magnolia trees blossom, and in the autumn when the ironwood tree, Japanese maple and tulip trees display their beautiful shades of yellow, orange and red. The National Trust arranges occasional events featuring walks to identify trees and flowers, craft exhibitions and Morris dancing.

Restormel Castle

From Lanhydrock's lower gate, a track follows the edge of Great Wood, leading to a footpath and narrow road along the side of the valley. Beyond the less than picturesque water works and rows of electricity pylons, there are fine views of the river flowing through tree-lined meadows where sheep and cattle graze. After a while, the silhouette of Restormel Castle appears above the trees where the side of the valley steepens.

Restormel is one of four Norman castles in Cornwall. It was built in the twelfth century by the Cardinham family. The original castle was built from wood, then rebuilt in stone at the end of the thirteenth century. Was it located and built primarily for defence or for its splendid views over what was then a deer park in the valley below? Despite its 17-m moat and the height and thickness of the castellated walls it has been suggested that, to a soldier's eye, other nearby sites would have been better. Its only experience of military action occurred during the Civil War when the Royalists forced the surrender of a Parliamentary garrison that had occupied it.

By the end of the Civil War, the castle was already considered a ruin. It was abandoned, and was completely hidden by trees and undergrowth until the end of the nineteenth century. It now belongs to English Heritage.

The castle retains a rugged nobility, set off by lawns, trees and shrubs. Enough remains for us to imagine what the original structure and life within it were like. The arched gate-

Restormel Castle from the flood plain

way leads into a grassy communal area, surrounded by walls with internal doorways and windows to the kitchens and other rooms. On top of the parallel inner and outer walls, is an almost complete circular walk around the battlements with fine views out over the Fowey Valley to the hills on its eastern side.

A Roman settlement has been found on the hill immediately to the south of Restormel. There seems to have been an ancient river crossing below the castle, near the Duchy of Cornwall's splendidly restored Restormel Manor, and the navigable tidal estuary might once have reached this far inland. Centuries of tin streaming on the moors brought massive quantities of silt to the upper reaches of the estuary, and gradually pushed the tide back to its present upper limit at Lostwithiel.

Lostwithiel to St Winnow

Lostwithiel's medieval bridge over the River Fowey

Along the six miles (10 km) from Lostwithiel to the river mouth, the character of the river changes dramatically, from an almost insignificant and easily bridged stream to an arm of the English Channel deep enough for sea-going ships. The estuary has three branches on its eastern side: the River Lerryn, Penpoll Creek and Pont Pill.

The upper part of the estuary is now a haven for wildlife and canoeists, but a closer look at its shores reveals an industrial past. Much of the western bank is hidden by the railway embankment; the main river and its branches are lined with the remains of old stone-built quays, jetties, fish stores, mills and lime-kilns, now abandoned and many accessible only by boat. Up the steep adjacent hillsides are areas of ancient woodlands, where signs of medieval coppicing can still be seen.

And higher again, farms that date from the early medieval period are adapting to the realities of modern life. Many have opened holiday cottages and other attractions, while some have specialized in organic production and other niche markets.

Not all of the estuary's industrial past has disappeared. Though passenger services stopped long ago, the railway line from Lostwithiel is used daily for transferring china clay to the Carn Point docks that dominate the western bank opposite Mixtow.

Kayaks in the upper estuary of the River Fowey

Lostwithiel

Lostwithiel is a surprising little town. The A390 main road sweeps around and through it, doing it no favours scenically, but Lostwithiel's fascinating history has left a rich heritage. The name originates from the charter of 1189, and is thought to come from the Cornish *Lostwyd-heyel* – 'the tail of the forest' – a derivation that can still be appreciated from high on the valley side to the south-east. The site of Lostwithiel has always been important as a bridging point across the river, but it was once the main port on the Fowey estuary. The town initially developed under the protection of Edmund, Earl of Cornwall, who lived in Restormel Castle a mile (2 km) to the north.

In the thirteenth and fourteenth centuries, Lostwithiel flourished as a port, as a stannary town controlling the local tin trade, and as the main administrative centre for Cornwall. But it gradually declined in importance as the estuary silted up. As the sixteenth-century traveller John Leland put it, the tide 'hath ebbid and flowen above Lostwithiel; but now it flowith not ful to the toun.' Navigation was restricted to barges instead of sea-going ships; local tin production declined, and the centre of tin trading moved further to the west.

The town suffered badly during the Civil War. In 1644, Parliamentary forces occupied Lostwithiel and damaged the church and other buildings, and the siege and eventual capture of the town by the Royalists traumatized the local population. Though works of fiction, Daphne du Maurier's *The King's General* and EV Thompson's *The Vagrant King* are based on historical research, and include vivid descriptions of brutality and suffering as the common soldiers at first abused the town and were then driven from it.

The early nineteenth-century revival of the mining industry brought new business to Lostwithiel as a port, with metal ore carried down from the Restormel iron mine and loaded on to barges for eventual transfer to larger ships in Fowey. Lime was shipped in the opposite direction, and carried by wagons from the lime kilns to fertilize the fields of the farming community.

Lostwithiel also benefited from the mainline railway, which arrived in 1859. Workshops were built in the town to produce materials used in constructing the line, its viaducts and stations; they continued in use for maintaining the rolling stock once goods and passenger services began. In 1869, the branch line that leads downriver to Fowey was opened; regular passenger services ceased in 1965, but the line is still in daily use by mineral trains and, very occasionally, to carry steam-train enthusiasts on what must be one of the most beautiful train rides in the country.

Some notable features of modern Lostwithiel are the medieval bridge, thought to have been built in the thirteenth century, and since lengthened on the eastern side to span the changing course of the river, and the nearby memorial to wartime heroes and victims. Further downriver, and set back from the site of the old town quay, are the stone walls and archway of the Duchy Palace. It was originally built in the thirteenth century, and served as the administrative centre for the county as well as for the tin industry. Cornwall's coat of arms can be seen on the northern wall.

Most of the church, which is dedicated to St Bartholomew, dates from the fourteenth century. Taprell House was built as a residence in the sixteenth century, with the adjoining Georgian extension, Edgecumbe House, added later. Taprell House was reno-

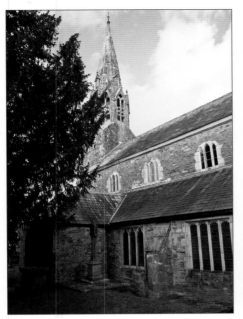

Clockwise from left: St Bartholomew's Church; the public library at Taprell House, and Walter Kendall's wall inscription, all in Lostwithiel

vated in the 1990s, and now houses the library. The strangely familiar Déjà-Vu is one of several antique shops in the town, and there are some pleasant, quiet restaurants.

An intriguing inscription on the cornerstone of a house on North Street reports that in 1652 Walter Kendall rather hopefully took a lease on a house for 3,000 years. With simi-

lar farsightedness, the modern community of Lostwithiel was an early convert to the 'transition town' concept, committing to a more self-sufficient future, less dependent on fossil fuels.

On the western bank of the River Fowey, at the southern edge of the town, near the railway bridge over the river, is a slipway for small boats, and beyond that Coulson Park,

opened in 1907 and financed by Nathaniel Coulson. He had been born into poverty in Lostwithiel in 1850, but worked his way to San Francisco; became a dentist, and made a fortune from buying and selling land.

Further downstream, beyond a quay where a few modern boats are moored, the river meanders between two areas of saltmarsh, Madderly Moor to the east and Shirehall Moor on the western bank. The 9.5 ha (23 acre) area that is now Shirehall Moor served as the town's refuse dump for many years, but was declared a Local Nature Reserve in 2007. Since then, the town council has begun to restore the land and conserve its wetland habitats, where egrets, ducks, herons and swans are the most commonly observed species. You can walk the entire length of Shirehall Moor, but you will risk getting wet feet if you stray from the path that follows its eastern side.

From Lostwithiel, you can follow footpaths and narrow, almost traffic-free country lanes to Fowey, a total walking distance of about six miles (10 km) on the western side of the estuary. The route passes from Coulson Park under the mineral railway, along the side of a

The River Fowey meanders between Shirehall Moor and Madderly Moor

valley between it and the main line, around Milltown Pill with its almost hidden boat-house, and under the Milltown Viaduct.

The Saints' Way

From here, the path joins the Saints' Way, which commemorates a route taken by sixth-century pilgrims from Wales and Ireland to Brittany and Spain. They crossed Corn-wall from the Camel estuary to avoid the dangerous sea passage around Land's End. It is now a recognized long-distance walk of 26 miles (42 km) from Padstow to Fowey. In this section, the route follows a 'sunken lane' between high hedges for most of the next two miles (3 km), and there is no clear view of the estuary until the descent past St Samp-son's Church and into Golant.

On the eastern side of the estuary, the first destination is the beautiful little river-side settlement of St Winnow. Approaching from Lostwithiel, a footpath passes down the side of a small valley, giving fine views of the estuary before entering woodland and winding its way towards the village between shrubs of holly and moss-covered earth embankments.

The almost-hidden boathouse near Milltown (top). The mineral railway opposite St Winnow (above)

The church at St Winnow reflected in the River Fowey

Here the estuary is 500 m wide, but even at high tide it is shallow outside its winding main channel, and small boats can easily run aground in the soft mud. There was once a ford known as Lantyan Passage, level with Lantyan Wood on the western shore.

St Winnow is a picturesque little place, in a beautiful setting beside the estuary. Listed in the Domesday Book as San Winnuc, it has just half a dozen houses, a boatyard, a farm museum that opens in the spring and summer, and a fine old church.

Autumn on the Fowey estuary at St Winnow Point (left). The churchyard at St Winnow (above)

The church was originally built in the twelfth century, probably on the site of an earlier Celtic monastery, though most of it was rebuilt 300 years later, and only part of the northern wall survives from the Norman period. Dedicated to St Winnocus, the church has some old stained glass windows and intricately carved wood in the rood screen and bench ends, all probably dating from the fifteenth and sixteenth centuries, and worth a close look. Angela du Maurier, Daphne's sister, is buried near the upper entrance to the churchyard, and the graves of the locally prominent Vivian family stand tall in the opposite corner.

The River Lerryn

The streams that eventually come together to form the River Lerryn rise to the south of the A390, and drain a large area of undulating, partly wooded but mainly agricultural countryside east of Lostwithiel. Much of the land belongs to Boconnoc, one of Cornwall's largest remaining estates, and public access is limited.

The Cornwall Spring Flower Show at Boconnoc

Boconnoc

Boconnoc appeared in the Domesday Book as Bochenod, and it has had an eventful history. One former owner was beheaded; three died in duels; one was charged with three separate murders and pardoned or acquitted each time. The original house was rebuilt by William Mohun in the sixteenth century, and has been remodeled several times. But the fifteenth-century church in the grounds has changed little. Boconnoc served briefly as the headquarters of King Charles I during the Civil War, and in 1643 and 1644 the two battles of Braddock Down were fought nearby.

In 1717, Thomas Pitt bought the estate, using the proceeds of the sale of a single diamond that he had acquired while serving as the Governor of Madras, in India. In 1771, Pitt's son erected an obelisk in memory of his wife's uncle, Sir Richard Lyttleton. It stands 38 m (123 ft) high, and its slender pinnacle can be seen above the trees from far beyond the estate boundary.

Since 1864, the estate has been owned by the Fortescue family. In the Second World War it was occupied by American troops, and was a local base in preparation for the D-Day

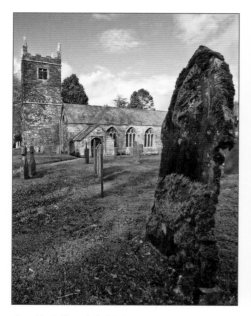

Braddock Church (left). Snowdrops in the churchyard at St Nectan's (right)

landings. The house and grounds fell into decline after 1969, but have been revived and renovated since 2001, regaining their place as a local landmark and centre of events.

About 100 head of deer roam the deer park at the lower end of the estate; 8 ha (20 acres) of gardens are filled with azaleas, camellias, rhododendrons and newly planted magnolias; softwood and a hardwood plant-

ing programmes are underway to recreate the original landscape plan, and the house and grounds have been used as locations for several films. The estate is open for garden visits each spring in support of various charities, and for an annual programme of events, of which the biggest and best known are the Cornwall Spring Flower Show in April and the Steam Fair in July.

Outside the estate there are few public footpaths, but a network of minor roads connect isolated farms and hamlets. They offer broad panoramas over patches of woodland, ploughed fields and pastures divided by traditional Cornish hedgerows, occasionally descending into deep, tree-lined valleys.

Braddock Church lies a little outside the Boconnoc boundary. Dedicated to St Mary, the font and parts of the building date from the Norman period; the square tower was added in the fifteenth century. The churchyard has an unusual gateway with a carved stone arch. Two miles (3 km) to the southwest, near the road up from Lostwithiel, is the chapel of St Nectan, or St Nighton, with its distinctively squat tower and tiled bell cot. Both churches present a peaceful, quietly confident face to the world, and the humble little St Nectan's has a heartening history of near-destruction, abandonment and renewal by a dedicated local community.

The lack of footpaths makes it difficult to follow the River Lerryn and the streams that flow into it before they pass under a bridge at Couch's Mill. From here, a minor road runs parallel to the river for just over a mile (2 km) until it flows under its final bridge at one of the most picturesque sites on the estuary, the village of Lerryn.

Lerryn

Boats and reflections at Lerryn

The present bridge was built in 1573, although there were others from as early as the thirteenth century. This is the highest point reached by the tide, and immediately after the bridge the riverbed widens dramatically. At low tide the stream meanders between wide banks of unattractive soft mud, crossed by stepping-stones. When the tide is at its highest on a sunny day, the calm water creates beautiful reflections of the surrounding woods, the cottages with their well-kept gardens, and a few moored boats, disturbed only by the graceful passage of ducks, swans and gulls.

Early settlers here were probably farmers and fishermen. In the sixteenth century, silver was carried from a nearby mine for smelting in the village. Barges brought lime up from Fowey to be burnt in four kilns, still visible along the river bank, although one is now a house. Lerryn's location up a long creek made it a good hiding place for smugglers, and in the eighteenth century there was a regular trade in brandy and other contraband.

The modern village has a primary school, a post office shop and a pub, the Ship Inn, which dates from the eighteenth century. The Red Store, with its distinctively painted doors, was built in about 1870 as a store-house, and is now a community centre. The slipway is a good place to launch a small boat, and canoes may be rented nearby. On a grassy area beside the river are picnic tables, where hikers and canoeists get ready for, or recover from, an exploration downriver.

On the hill behind the school is an interesting hedge. At a glance, it is like any other hedge, 1–2 m (3–6 ft) high, grown over, with the occasional tree; but this hedge continues almost unbroken to Lanreath, and from there intermittently to Looe, eight miles (13 km) away. In places it is more than 3 m high and,

Paddling upriver past Ethy Quay at Lerryn

The remains of a fountain in Tivoli Park, Lerryn (left). The boathouse at Penquite Quay (right)

according to Arthur Quiller-Couch's story *The Mayor of Troy*, wide enough for a platoon of soldiers to march along the top.

This is the Giant's Hedge, or the Devil's Hedge as Quiller-Couch calls it, which is thought to have been built soon after the Roman period to mark the northern boundary of a Cornish kingdom. Some believe the hedge continued further west across the Fowey estuary as far as Castle Dore, above the village of Golant. It is sometimes difficult to identify on the ground, but one of the best preserved sections is in Willake Wood, about half a mile (1 km) to the east of Lerryn.

Another fragment of history in Lerryn is Tivoli Park, laid out by the china clay magnate

Frank Parkyn in about 1920. The name probably originates from an amusement park that Parkyn visited in Copenhagen. What is left of the park can still be seen near the southern bank of the River Lerryn, a little downriver from the village, but not much more than a sculpted fountain and some untended ornamental plants remains.

Some beautiful walks start or end in Lerryn, with footpaths leading both up and down the river valley. A circular route passes down the northern bank to St Winnow Point, where there is a wonderful view southwards over a broad section of the estuary towards Golant; then north to St Winnow and back over the hill, passing St Winnow Mill.

On the outward leg, this route passes through Ethy Wood, an ancient broadleaved woodland where coppice management is still evident. Below, Ethy Quay is a small, rocky and low-lying part of the river bank that extends into the channel of the River Lerryn near a small inlet. There was once a boathouse here, built by an owner of Ethy Manor in the nineteenth century, but little remains of it now. Instead, this has become a favourite stopping place for walkers who step down from the pathway and let their dogs run in the water, and for families who photograph each other lounging on the rocks.

On the opposite bank, a little downstream, is another flat promontory near the remains of a quarry, which has a stranger history. During the Napoleonic wars, a number of French prisoners were held captive nearby, and a group of them escaped and made this their hiding place. Cathy Parkes' excellent *Historic Audit of the Fowey Estuary* refers to this point as 'France', and Wilson Macarthur was told it was 'Frenchman's Island'.

There is much speculation that this area inspired Kenneth Grahame's classic *The Wind in the Willows*. Grahame stayed nearby; and by common consent the woods have a timeless, almost magical quality. So it is often suggested that Ethy Manor on the hill above the river could be Toad Hall, and the novel's Wild Woods might be Ethy Wood and The Great Wood alongside the estuary below Lerryn.

Opposite St Winnow Point, on the western shore of the estuary, is Penquite Quay boathouse. Perhaps because of its Italian design it is sometimes mistakenly identified with Giuseppe Garibaldi, the Italian patriot. He befriended Colonel John Peard, who fought in the Italian liberation campaign and owned Penquite. The house is on the hill above the estuary and is now a youth hostel.

As part of a triumphal tour of southern England, Garibaldi visited Penquite in 1864 – attracting crowds of several thousands, according to the *Royal Cornwall Gazette*, disrupting train services and paralysing shops and businesses for two days. In *The Parish of Golant*, published in 1885, EW Rashleigh wrote: 'It was feared that Garibaldi's stay in England might bring us into difficulties abroad. To get rid of him the Duke of Sutherland's yacht steamed into Fowey harbour, and took him away from Penquite back to Italy.'

In fact, the boathouse was built in 1890, but it has an intriguing history. Frank Parkyn now owned Penquite. He was friendly with the Prince of Wales, later King Edward VII. The Prince visited on a number of occasions, and as a plaque on the boathouse puts it, 'besported himself with young ladies'. The boathouse is accessible only by boat, and a notice warns that it is a sanctuary for adders.

Golant and Castle Dore

Boats at low tide near Golant

The village of Golant has grown up where a local stream flows down a narrow, steep-sided and wooded valley and into an inlet or pill on the western shore of the estuary. Historically, this has been an area of fruit orchards, cider-making and fishing, and the quay was used for landing limestone, sand and seaweed to fertilize local farmland. A little upstream there was an ancient ford across to the hamlet of Cliff on the eastern bank, used in 1644 by King Charles to outflank the Parliamentary army. The ford was defended from a gun emplacement still to be found in the undergrowth above the eastern shore.

The railway embankment separated Golant Pill from the main stream, creating a harbour where most of the local boats are moored. But even with the intrusion of the railway, Rashleigh described Golant in 1885 as 'nestling amidst its plum trees and apple orchards, undisturbed by troubles of the outside world – the admiration of all who go there for its peaceful, quiet look.'

Since then, things have changed as pubs, a school, a village hall, a railway station and a boat-building business have opened and closed, houses have been modernized and more have been built, together with a 'human sundial' near the boat landing. Now the main attractions for outsiders are the Fisherman's Arms and the Cormorant Hotel, and the river itself.

The numbers of pleasure boats moored on the reach beyond the railway have grown rapidly in recent years. The receding tide reveals a wide expanse of reddish sand broken by pools and channels patrolled by egrets, with the boats tethered to their mooring buoys, stranded and lifeless. But on a calm day when the tide is high, the views

Spring flowers at St Sampson's Church (above); inside the church (right)

out over the water are as good as ever, and visiting the modern village feels like a retreat from ordinary life.

The original settlement of Golant owes a great deal to its location on the Saints Way. Among the early pilgrims was St Sampson, who stayed nearby while travelling to Brittany during the sixth century. He established a church on the site of an old Celtic hermitage on a hill to the north of the village overlooking the estuary. The present building dates from the early sixteenth century, and is dedicated to St Sampson, who is depicted in some of the stained glass windows.

St Sampson's is yet another delightful, peaceful little country church within the Fowey Valley. It has a holy well beside the door; a set of five bells; a pipe organ, and, according to John Betjeman, the least comfortable pews of any church in England. Like its nearest neighbour at St Winnow, St Sampson's is a Grade I listed building. And carved into the lower gates to the churchyard are two inscriptions: 'Tristan' and 'Iseult'.

Tristan and Iseult

The legend of Tristan and Iseult originated from one or other of two twelfth-century poems, one by Thomas of Brittany and the other by the Anglo-Norman poet Béroul, both probably based in turn on an earlier work in either the Cornish or Breton language. There are versions of the story in several European languages, all of which are long and include many convoluted twists and turns. It has sometimes been incorporated into the legend of King Arthur, and into the legends of other nations. But at heart it is a story of adventure, romance and tragedy, based around three main characters: the fifth-century Cornish King Mark, his nephew or adopted son Tristan, and the beautiful Irish princess Iseult.

It is impossible to say how much of the story is based on real people and historical events, and where these events might have taken place. The Golant area has as good a claim as anywhere, based partly on place names in the legend that have local equivalents. Apple orchards occur in most versions of the story, and were a traditional feature of farms around the Fowey estuary. Then there are Castle Dore and the 'Tristan Stone'.

What remains of Castle Dore is a roughly circular pattern of earthworks, about a mile (2 km) west of Golant beside the road to Fowey. Similar to the structures up the valley at Berry Castle and Bury Castle, these are thought to have enclosed a village prior to the Roman period. More intriguingly, excavations in the 1930s revealed evidence of a large wooden building dating from the sixth century. Nearby, a long stone was found bearing an inscription, unreadable except by experts, that refers to King Mark. The stone now stands beside the road to Fowey, near Four Turnings. Its discovery led to the suggestion that Castle Dore was the home of King Mark, and so of the Tristan and Iseult legend.

More recent research suggests King Mark lived a little further north, near the present-day farms of Castle or Lantyan. Wherever he lived, it was probably in a wooden building whose remains are unlikely to be traced.

The story of Tristan and Iseult has inspired a long list of works in the world of the arts. Richard Wagner wrote the opera *Tristan und Isolde* that was first performed in 1863. Alfred Tennyson, Matthew Arnold and others have written poems, short stories and novels that draw on the legend, which has also served as the basis for a number of films, most recently *Tristan + Isolde*, which appeared in 2006.

Castle Dore earthworks (above). The Tristan Stone at Four Turnings above Fowey (right)

Arthur Quiller-Couch wrote the first half of a novel that recreates the story in a Victorian setting, and includes some fine descriptions of the local landscape. Looking across to the far side of the valley towards St Winnow, for example, one of the main characters saw a breathtaking view below, of 'the placid river, and across it and glassed in it on the brim of the farther shore, a grey church set among elms overlooking a tiny quay. The woodland above and to left and right shone over the water exquisitely mirrored.' If Quiller-Couch were to visit on a calm, sunlit morning now he could write exactly the same sentence.

The novel includes recognizable descriptions of journeys up and down the estuary, in and out of creeks like Woodget Pyll (Woodgate Pill), and between familiar lo-cal landmarks including Troytown (Fowey), Castle Dor (spelled thus), a field called Mark's Gate, Milltown, Penquite and, sup-posedly most significant for the legend, Lan-tyan, now a picturesque stone farmhouse to whose owners the book is dedicated. Quiller-Couch left the book unfinished, but his daughter persuaded Daphne du Maurier to complete it, and in 1962 it was published under her name as *Castle Dor*.

Penpoll Creek

Ramparts of the castle at Bury Down, Lanreath, and the view to the west (left). The upper section of the valley of Trebant Water on a sunny winter morning (right)

Penpoll Creek joins the estuary a little downstream from Golant, and on the opposite side. It is fed by Trebant Water, which rises six miles (10 km) to the north-east, below Bury Down and to the north of Lanreath. Of all the valleys that feed into the Fowey estuary, this is probably the least well served by public footpaths. But it is not inaccessible.

An obvious modern feature of Bury Down is a communications mast that can be seen from many miles away. A little to the west and below the mast are the remains of what the Cornwall Archaeological Unit describes as 'an excellent example of an Iron Age hillslope fort.' This is private land, and access is by permission of Botelet Farm.

The inner ramparts are almost circular, about 2 m high and 90 m across, clearly visible from the north as an irregularity on the smoothly curved outline of the hillside. The view from the top is as stunning as we have come to expect from ancient sites like this: it extends from the tors of Bodmin Moor to the north, west across the valley of the River Fowey and its tributaries, and south to the coast as far as St Austell Bay and Dodman Point.

The entrance to Penpoll Creek

Trebant Water flows to the south and west through a narrow, often steep-sided valley, accessible here and there by winding country lanes, and past farms old enough to appear in the Domesday Book, but evolving quickly to reduce their dependence on traditional agriculture. Botelet Farm, Porfell Farm and the Shillamill Lakes offer not only accommodation for visitors, but also fishing and educational facilities for local history, agriculture and the environment.

Penpoll Creek is a peaceful place, with broadleaf woods on either side for much of its length, and flocks of seabirds on the mud banks. Though it is now little disturbed by people, a few abandoned quays show where

A waterfall near St Cadix Priory on Penpoll Creek

the slipway beside the bridge at Middle Pen-poll or from Golant or Lerryn. Walkers can reach the foreshore on public footpaths at three places: near the head of the creek at Lower Penpoll; within the Lombard National Trust area on the south bank, from a path that leads down from the road to Mixtow; and at St Cyric's Creek, near the site of the old St Cadix Priory, now restored as a modern residence. There is a pretty little waterfall beside the footpath, but beware! It is difficult to cross the stream without getting wet feet.

Above Penpoll Creek, on its northern bank, is the hamlet of St Veep, and another example of a modestly beautiful little Cornish country church. Most of the present building dates from the fourteenth and fifteenth centuries; the carved granite font is early fifteenth century, and the earliest slate epitaphs inside date from the sixteenth century. There is yew and holly in the churchyard, and, in March, snowdrops among the gravestones.

The 17 m (55-ft), two-stage tower houses six bells, perhaps the church's proudest feature. When recast in 1770, with silver coins thrown into the molten metal to improve the tone, they emerged from their moulds in perfect pitch – a 'maiden peal' requiring no retuning. Bell-ringing is still important, and several entries in the visitors' book are from ringers.

farmers once unloaded lime to fertilize their fields. Near one of them, the ribs of a long-forgotten boat poke up through the mud. A few modern vessels are moored near the entrance to the creek, and half-way along it someone has anchored a floating summerhouse in the meandering stream channel.

The creek is best explored when the tide is up, in a small boat, launched perhaps from

Pont Pill

Mist and frost on a March morning near Lanreath

Pont Pill creek is fed by a stream that flows down from the village of Lanreath, recorded as Lanredoch in the Domesday Book. Its fine old Punch Bowl Inn dates from the seventeenth century, and nearby is a row of 300-year-old cob cottages that were originally thatched. But Lanreath's main asset is its splendid church, St Marnarch's.

A gig team practises on the sunlit waters of Pont Pill

that leads into the tower. Here, beside the ropes that hang from the six bells, are posters from bell-ringing festivals that local ringers have taken part in or hosted.

From Lanreath, a lane, footpath and bridle-way make a pleasant walk all the way to Pont, parallel to the stream and including a mile (2 km) on its banks through a wood above Porthpean House. The route passes near Trethake Mill, now a private house, where the waterwheel has been modified to generate electricity. This is an example of the unusual 'pitchback' design, where the water falls on to the wheel from above, but drives it anti-clockwise, so it appears to rotate backwards.

Like Penpoll Creek and Lerryn, the upper part of Pont Pill consists of little more than mud banks for much of the time, until the tide flows in. A picturesque group of stone cottages huddles around the quay and footbridge near the tidal limit; swans and ducks cruise sedately back and forth, on the lookout for food from passersby. A notice preserved from 1894 setting out 'dues for discharging or shipping over these quays' – a penny per quarter of grain, threepence per ton of manure – recalls a more industrial past.

The oldest part of the building dates from the early twelfth century. Among its most notable features are the Norman font, with its beautifully carved conical wooden cover; the carved wood panels on some of the bench ends and the Elizabethan pulpit; a fine monument to the Grylls family, of whom five members served successively as rectors from 1614 to 1736; and the fifteenth-century arch

The footbridge marks the halfway point on the Hall Walk between Bodinnick and

St Wyllow Church, Lanteglos (above); the font with its carved cover (right)

Polruan. For most of its length, this splendid route follows the top of the tree-lined valley sides, with occasional glimpses of the creek far below, where you might see a group of sea kayaks exploring, or one of the local gig-rowing teams practising.

A real gem lies at the end of the footpath that passes up the narrow tributary valley to the south of the footbridge. Simon Jenkins complains that 'those who can find this church deserve a medal', though ironically he describes Lanteglos-by-Fowey as having a 'hilltop location'. More importantly, he admires its restored woodwork and awards it two stars.

Viewed from above on the coast road between Polruan and Polperro, its granite tower rises clear above the surrounding trees.

The church is dedicated to St Wyllow, a sixth-century Irish saint who is supposed to have been decapitated but managed to carry his head for half a mile (1 km) to the site of the present building, where he was buried. The only house nearby is Churchtown Farm, so the majority of attenders must travel for a mile (2 km) or so from Polruan.

Most of the building dates from the four-teenth century, though much restoration work was carried out about 100 years ago.

Sailing boats moored in Pont Pill

The octagonal Norman font is carved from local Pentewan stone, and a now-familiar plaque presented by Charles II recognizes the community's loyalty during the English Civil War. Aside from the carved bench ends that Simon Jenkins admired, the church has an impressive brass memorial to one of the Mohun family, the local medieval land-owners from the fourteenth century. Outside, the tower and its accompanying yew trees overlook graves that have been cut into the hillside, marked by polished granite and slate headstones, and interspersed with seasonal wildflowers.

Polruan

The top of the hill overlooking the English Channel seems an unlikely place for Polruan's earliest settlement, yet it is here that St Ruan is supposed to have lived. It is certainly the site of the earliest chapel in the area. St Saviour's dates from the eighth century, though it was enlarged 700 years later. It served as a navigation mark for ships, and as a lookout to warn of approaching enemies. All that remains of the original St Saviour's now is part of a well-buttressed wall beside the coastguard station.

Polruan from Hall Walk

The centre of modern Polruan is at the bottom and on the landward-side of the hill, clustered around a north-facing bay near the mouth of the estuary, and sheltered from the prevailing winds. The only way into the village, aside from walking from Pont Pill or along the coast, is down a steep and narrow road that leads directly to the main quay, a handful of small shops and cafés, the neighbouring Russell and Lugger inns, and the passenger ferry to Fowey.

Polruan was originally a fishing village, and what is now the Harbour Commissioner's office was built as a processing factory for pilchards, or sardines, once a staple product of every community along this stretch of coast. But the village became better known for building boats and small ships. Vessels weighing a grand total of more than 6,000 tons were launched from here during the nineteenth century.

The main boatyard that remains active is C Toms & Son, which repairs and refits sea-going ships and builds new ones, including some of the pilot boats that guide china clay freighters and cruisers in and out of the harbour. Toms' slipway, workshops and storage yards take up much of Polruan's waterfront,

A three-masted sailing ship under repair at Toms' Yard, Polruan

and create an impression of hard graft and industry that has gone from other parts of the estuary.

On a promontory at the western end of Polruan are the well-preserved remains of the Blockhouse, a square, utilitarian structure of thick stone walls built in the fourteenth century. It was linked to its twin on the Fowey side by a chain that could be raised to keep out enemy ships.

Further round on the seaward side of the point is Headland Garden, a privately owned refuge that has become one of Polruan's most attractive features, though it is open for only limited periods during the summer months. Monterey pines and other exotic, sub-

Polruan: The Blockhouse and moored sailing boats on a sunlit early-autumn morning (above); spring flowers in Headland Gardens (right)

tropical plants seem to grow directly from the rocks, somehow surviving regular buffetings from south-westerly gales. On a clear day, there are wonderful views to Gribben Head and Dodman Point. A long stairway leads down to a cove where visitors may bathe.

The Town of Fowey

The town quay and church from across the estuary

In *The Story of Fowey*, John Keast creates a picture of a town that has seen dramatic and sometimes violent changes of fortune over the centuries. Fowey had little significance during the Norman period; but by the fourteenth century, as silt began to choke the upper parts of the estuary, the centre of local commerce had shifted from Lostwithiel, and Fowey became one of the leading ports on the entire south coast of England. In 1346 its contribution of ships and men to the siege of Calais was the largest of any English port.

It was not only legitimate trade and military activity that brought in new wealth. Writing in 1907, Arthur Norway observed that, under the Plantagenets, 'most naval warfare was curiously like piracy', and the leading local families regularly acted on both sides of the law. Mark Michaelstow (or Mixtow) was one of the more notorious adventurers, sometimes in support of the King and sometimes against; and there are many tales of Fowey men seizing foreign ships both within the harbour and in the sea lanes outside.

These activities invited retaliation, usually by the French, Spanish or Dutch, and sometimes from further afield. In 1621, a group of local men were abducted by 'Turkish' pirates and sold into slavery in Algiers. The worst attack occurred in 1457, when a large French force made a surprise raid and destroyed much of the town. The dam-

The town of Fowey from Hall Walk

age, together with continued silting of the river and the westward shift in the tin trade, hastened Fowey's decline in relation to Plymouth and other south-west ports.

The Civil War brought more hardship, from the fighting and because most of the prominent local families supported the King and were forced to pay huge fines during the Commonwealth period of the 1650s. The town revived with the restoration of Charles II, the growth of fishing and smuggling, and active involvement in the Napoleonic Wars, but declined again soon afterwards. In 1853, a traveller described 'a lamentably wasted town', whose beautiful natural setting was marred by streets full of rubbish.

Low tide on the beach at Readymoney Cove (left). The Polruan passenger ferry (right)

Since then, Fowey has been transformed by the railway, shipbuilding, china clay, and, more recently, the arrival of writers, artists and tourists, and the explosion in the numbers of pleasure boats. Late in the Victorian period, and in the early years of the twentieth century, the town expanded rapidly, back up the hill towards the imposing Fowey Hall, and southwards towards the old Rashleigh family home at Point Neptune above Readymoney Cove.

Boating is the estuary's main attraction, and sailing remains almost synonymous with Fowey. The distinctive, locally designed wooden Troy class sailing boats still race regularly, though in a setting very different from when the early ones were built in the 1930s and 1940s. Rows of yellow mooring buoys now partition much of the estuary – empty in winter, fully subscribed through the summer.

Perhaps because of the sailing, the lack of a large beach, or its inability to absorb much traffic within its narrow streets, Fowey has avoided most of the twentieth-century brashness that has overtaken other Cornish coastal towns.

And once on the water, there is still a sense of a small world that is distinct from life on land. This is the world of the ferrymen at Polruan and Bodinnick; the crews of the tugs and pilot boats that shepherd ocean-going freighters and cruise ships in and out of the harbour; the water taxis taking visiting sailors to their moorings; the harbourside sailmakers and boatyards; the harbourmaster crossing back and forth in his launch, and the groups

Red sails on the estuary by Pont Pill (above).
The font and nave of St Fimbarrus church (right)

of a dozen or so on the otherwise deserted foreshore along by Wiseman's Reach, hauling ropes seemingly hundreds of metres long to bring in a catch of sand eels.

Even so, the crowds of visitors during summer weekends are, frankly, overwhelming and best avoided. Spring and autumn are ideal for sampling the bakeries, art galleries and bookshops on Fore Street, and the pubs and restaurants that open on to the harbour.

Church of St Fimbarrus

The church, dedicated to St Fimbarrus, is a less prominent feature of Fowey than you might expect, considering that its tower is the second highest of any parish church in Cornwall. It was built into the hill above the Town Quay; it is overlooked by rows of houses above, and it is close to the battlements of Place, the home of the Treffry family since the fifteenth century, whose tower rises even higher. But the elegant structure that we see today reflects a fascinating history.

St Fimbarrus lived in Ireland, and died there in the year 630. The church guide describes his connection with Fowey as 'tenuous', most likely only that he followed the Saints Way and passed through Fowey on one of his trips to Rome.

The original church on this site was probably small and simple, built beside a stream that still flows through a culvert under the pathway beside the south wall. The church was rebuilt by the Normans in about 1150, then fell into disrepair and was rebuilt again almost 200 years later. But the raid on the town in 1457 caused so much damage that the church had to be rebuilt yet again. The work was not finished until the start of the next century, and since then there have been relatively minor changes, mainly internal, including the handsome Delabole slate floor that was laid in 1996.

Inside, the first impression is of a spacious interior, well lit from the stained glass in the eastern wall and the clerestory windows above the arches on each side of the nave. Together they illuminate the beautiful wagon-style roof, with its plastered ceiling covered by a lattice of exposed timbers. There are fine examples of carved wood panels in the pulpit and on the delicate, open screen at the chancel steps. Several stone, wood and brass memorials around the walls commemorate members of leading local families, most notably the Treffrys and Rashleighs, each of which has its own chapel at the eastern end of the church. The carved stone font in the entrance to the tower is the only remnant of the original Norman church.

The tower houses eight bells, two of which were added after the eighteenth-century picture of the ringers was painted on a board mounted on the wall beside the bell ropes. Below the painting, a poem warns that each ringer who swears, curses, presents himself in a bad mood or 'by unskilffull handling marrs a Peal' will be expected to pay a sixpenny fine, 'twill make him cautious gainst another time'.

Writers and artists

There is probably no part of Cornwall with stronger literary connections than those in the lower part of the Fowey estuary. Sir Arthur Quiller-Couch lived in Fowey, and used the town as the setting for his Troytown novels, which provide a charming, whimsical glimpse into nineteenth-century Cornish life. Locally known as 'Q', for several years

Prime Cellars, on the eastern side of the Fowey estuary, downstream from Bodinnick

he took possession of Prime Cellars, the oddly misshapen one-storey building on the eastern side of the estuary downstream from Bodinnick. In his short story about the house, he called it *Priam's Cellars*. High above it, a granite obelisk commemorates his work, at a point on the Hall Walk that commands one of the best views of the lower estuary.

Quiller-Couch befriended Kenneth Grahame, who often visited, and from the Fowey Hotel he wrote some of the letters to his son that he eventually expanded to become *The Wind in the Willows*. There is nothing in the story that is distinctly Cornish, and the setting is more likely to have been the Thames, where Grahame spent much of his child-

The 'Q' memorial on Hall Walk, above the estuary

town I know so well, that clings along one steep side of the harbour. There through the dark doorways you look down flights of stone steps, overhung by great pink tufts of valerian and ending in a patch of sparkling blue water … the salmon leap on the flood tide, schools of mackerel flash and play past quaysides.'

Quiller-Couch also served as an early mentor for Daphne du Maurier, who lived most of her adult life on or near the estuary. Her first local home was at Ferryside, beside the Bodinnick ferry landing on the east bank. She was married in Lanteglos church, and the town of Fowey and other local places feature in all her Cornish novels.

The Loving Spirit revolves around a boatyard in Polruan. As we saw earlier, *The King's General* records the ebb and flow of the Civil War across this part of Cornwall, and *Castle Dor* is set in the hamlets, farms and fine old houses around the village of Golant. The town of Fowey appears, at least tangentially, in each of *Frenchman's Creek*, *Rebecca* and *The House on the Strand*.

The Daphne du Maurier Festival, held around the time of her birthday in May, is one of the town's biggest regular events. It draws nationally known writers and broadcasters as part of a ten-day programme of talks, exhibitions and walks.

hood. But his experiences around Fowey and Lerryn probably inspired him, and in a beautifully written passage, an adventurous stranger makes a brief appearance.

He is a Sea Rat about to embark on a long journey that Grahame must have taken often, towards the south-west and a 'little grey

The entrance to Fowey harbour… with apologies to Turner

Other well-known writers who once lived and worked beside the Fowey estuary were Leo Walmsley, whose novel *Love in the Sun* is based on his experiences living in an old army hut on Pont Pill near Polruan; and Denys Val Baker who lived in a secluded, seventeenth-century house on Bodmin Pill and wrote about it in *Life up the Creek*. The house was originally a sawmill, and is now an internationally known music recording studio, still accessible only by boat at high tide, or from the Saints' Way footpath that passes nearby.

Modern Fowey is as notable for its art galleries as its writers, and local artists have some illustrious predecessors. Sometime in 1811, JMW Turner climbed down to the bottom of the cliffs below where the Fowey Hotel now stands, sketched the view towards the sea, and eventually made two paintings based on the sketch. Entitled *The Entrance of Fowey Harbour*, the paintings show the now-ruined Fowey blockhouse prominent on the right, its Polruan twin on the left, and St Catherine's Point in the distance.

The Coast

St Catherine's Point: The Rashleigh mausoleum (left) and the castle (right)

To end this exploration of the Fowey Valley, continue south along the Esplanade, beyond Readymoney Cove and on to the Rashleigh mausoleum and the castle at St Catherine's Point, or up to a bench in Allday's Field. Take a good look back up the estuary, across the harbour mouth to the little white Punches Cross on the rocks below Polruan's Headland Garden, and out to the English Channel in one of its many moods.

A summer view of Pont Pill, the mouth of the estuary and St Austell Bay

These are views that cross the centuries, shared by small boys who gazed in wonder at 47 vessels sailing out to join Edward III at the siege of Calais 650 years ago; watchmen fearful of raiding pirates from France or the Mediterranean; anxious mothers waiting for overdue sailing ships; exhausted soldiers who might have glimpsed the Earl of Essex slipping away and along the coast to Plymouth in 1644, and wives and grandfathers who waved at gunboats and troop carriers heading for Normandy 300 years later.

Reflect on the sadness of it all. But, above all, be uplifted by the raw, timeless beauty of what you see.

Index

Note: References in *italic* are to illustrations.